CHRISTIANICA

Christianica

The Basic Teachings
of the
Christian Faith
arranged for
Prayer
and
Meditation

CHRISTIANICA CENTER
6 NORTH MICHIGAN AVENUE
CHICAGO ILLINOIS 60602

Library of Congress Catalog Card Number: 74-13005
International Standard Book Number: 0-911346-02-3

The Scripture quotations in this publication are from the Revised Standard Version Common Bible, copyright 1973 by the Division of Christian Education, National Council of Churches of Christ in the U.S.A. and used by permission.

The Revised Standard Version Common Bible, from which the quotations in this book have been taken, has been endorsed or approved by:

Francis Cardinal Koenig, Archbishop of Vienna
President of the World Catholic Federation
for the Biblical Apostolate

The Reverend Dr. Gerald E. Knoff
Associate General Secretary for Christian Education
National Council of Churches of Christ in the U.S.A.

Archbishop Athenagoras of Thyateira and Great Britain
Exarch of the Ecumenical Patriarchate of Constantinople

Manufactured in the United States of America
Second Printing: November, 1975

Contents

The Thirty Meditations of the *Christianica*

Part I The Prelude

Part II The Metanoia

Part III The Paradox

Part IV The Challenge

Part V The Climax

Part VI The Triumph

What the *Christianica* Is

The *Christianica* is a prayer which presents the basic teachings of the Christian Faith in a series of 30 "Meditations." Half of the Meditations are devoted to the religious and moral doctrine taught by Jesus. The other 15 Meditations describe the principal events in the history of our salvation, such as the Incarnation, the Crucifixion, and the Resurrection. Each Meditation includes an introductory prayer, ten related scriptural quotations, a refrain, and a concluding antiphon.

How to Pray the *Christianica*

The *Christianica* is not meant to be read; it is meant to be prayed and meditated upon. For this reason each scriptural verse of each Meditation is followed by a "refrain" which is itself another scriptural verse. The refrain emphasizes the mood of the Meditation and causes your attention to linger in fuller appreciation of the verse you have just read.

Let us say that you are about to pray the Thirteenth Meditation, "Riches." Begin by praying the Lord's Prayer (Our Father . . .) as an introduction to the Meditation. Then read or recite the first verse:

Jesus declared, 'How hard it is for those who have riches/
to enter the kingdom of God!'

Luke 18:24

Think about the significance of this verse as you pray the refrain:

Keep your life free
from love of money,/
for the love of money
is the root of all evils.

Heb 13:5; 1 Tim 6:10

Then read the second verse of the Meditation:

'For it is easier for a camel to go through the eye of a needle/
than for a rich man to enter the kingdom of God.'

Luke 18:25

Think about this second verse as you pray the refrain again (be sure to pray the *complete* refrain even though only the first line is reprinted):

Keep your life free ~

Continue in this manner for each of the remaining verses of the Meditation.

Then recite the concluding antiphon:

Be content with what you have;/
for has not God chosen those
who are poor in the world
to be rich in faith
and heirs of the kingdom
which he has promised
to those who love him?

Heb 13:5; Jas 2:5

Amen.

For Two People or a Group:

The *Christianica* has also been arranged as a balanced, alternating prayer. Each verse, each refrain, and each concluding antiphon is divided into two distinct parts by a slash mark (/). One person, or one section of a prayer group, may recite the first part, and the rest of the group may recite the second part.

When to Pray the Christianica:

Pray one Meditation each day and you will complete the 30 Meditations each month. Or pray five Meditations each day, beginning Monday, and you will complete the 30 Meditations on Saturday.

Part I The Prelude

The First Meditation CREATION AND THE FALL OF MAN

The Second Meditation THE LAW AND THE PROPHETS

The Third Meditation THE INCARNATION

The Fourth Meditation THE NATIVITY

The Fifth Meditation THE PRECURSOR

Each Meditation of the Christianica *begins with the prayer Jesus taught us:*

Our Father who art in heaven,
hallowed be thy name.
Thy kingdom come, thy will be
done, on earth as it is in
heaven./
Give us this day our daily bread;
and forgive us our trespasses,
as we forgive those who
trespass against us;
and lead us not into temptation,
but deliver us from evil.
Matt 6:9-13

Many people add:

For thine is the kingdom, and the
power, and the glory, for ever.

Amen.

The First Meditation

Creation and the Fall of Man

Our ✳ Father

In the beginning God created the heavens and the earth, and the fish of the sea, and the birds of the air, and the cattle, and every living thing that moves upon the earth./

And God saw everything that he had made, and behold, it was very good.

Gen 1:1, 26, 28, 31

Lord, when I look ✳ at thy heavens,
the work of thy fingers,
the moon and the stars
which thou hast established;/
what is man
that thou art mindful of him?

Psalm 8:1, 3, 4

And God created man in his own image; male and female he created them./

And God blessed them, saying, 'Be fruitful and multiply; and have dominion over every living thing upon the earth.'

Gen 1:27, 28

Lord, when I look ✳ at thy heavens ~

Lord, when I look at thy heavens,
the work of thy fingers,
the moon and the stars
which thou hast established;/
what is man
that thou art mindful of him?

And the LORD God planted a garden in Eden,/
and out of the ground he made to grow every tree that is pleasant to the sight and good for food.

Gen 2:8, 9

LORD, when I look ✳ at thy heavens ~

And he commanded, 'You may freely eat of every tree of the garden;/
but of the tree of the knowledge of good and evil you shall not eat, for in the day that you eat of it you shall die.'

Gen 2:16, 17

LORD, when I look ✳ at thy heavens ~

But the serpent said to the woman, 'You will not die./
For God knows that when you eat of it your eyes will be opened, and you will be like God, knowing good and evil.'

Gen 3:4, 5

LORD, when I look ✳ at thy heavens ~

Now the woman saw that the tree was good for food, and that it was a delight to the eyes,/
and that the tree was to be desired to make one wise.

Gen 3:6

LORD, when I look ☀ at thy heavens,
the work of thy fingers,
the moon and the stars
which thou hast established;/
what is man
that thou are mindful of him?

And she took of its fruit and ate;/
and she also gave some to her husband, and he ate.

Gen 3:6

LORD, when I look ☀ at thy heavens ~

Then the eyes of both were opened, and they knew that they were naked;/
and they hid themselves from the presence of the LORD God.

Gen 3:7, 8

LORD, when I look ☀ at thy heavens ~

Then the LORD God said to the serpent,
'Because you have done this, I will put enmity between you and the woman, and between your seed and her seed;/
he shall bruise your head, and you shall bruise his heel.'

Gen 3:14, 15

LORD, when I look ✳ at thy heavens ~

And to Adam he said, 'In the sweat of your face you shall eat bread till you return to the ground; you are dust, and to dust you shall return.'/
And he clothed them and sent them forth from the garden.

Gen 3:17, 19, 21, 23

LORD, when I look ✳ at thy heavens ~

Yet thou hast made him
little less than the angels,
and given him dominion
over the works of thy hands;/
thou hast put all things
under his feet.

Ps 8:5, 6; Heb 2:7

Amen.

The Second Meditation

THE LAW AND THE PROPHETS

Our ✡ Father

In those days the LORD said to Abraham, 'Because you have obeyed my voice your reward shall be very great./
You shall be the father of a great and mighty nation, and by you and your descendants shall all the families of the earth bless themselves.'

Gen 12:1, 22:18, 15:1, 17:4, 18:18, 28:14

LORD, give me ✡ understanding,/
that I may keep thy law
and observe it with my whole heart.

Psalm 119:34

Now after the people of Israel had gone forth out of the land of Egypt, the LORD called to Moses,/
saying, 'Tell the people: If you will obey my voice and keep my covenant, you shall be to me a kingdom of priests and a holy nation.'

Ex 19:1, 3, 5, 6

LORD, give me ✡ understanding ~

And God spoke all these words, saying, 'I am the LORD your God, who brought you out of the land of Egypt, out of the house of bondage./
You shall have no other gods before me.'
Ex 20:1-3

LORD, give me ✡ understanding ~

'You shall not take the name of the LORD your God in vain./
Observe the sabbath day, to keep it holy.'
Deut 5:11, 12

LORD, give me ✡ understanding ~

'Honor your father and your mother./
You shall not kill. Neither shall you commit adultery. Neither shall you steal.'
Deut 5:16-19

LORD, give me ✡ understanding ~

'You shall not bear false witness against your neighbor./
Neither shall you covet your neighbor's wife; and you shall not desire your neighbor's house, his field, his ox, or anything that is your neighbor's.'
Ex 20:16; Deut 5:21

LORD, give me ✡ understanding ~

And the people said, 'All that the LORD has spoken we will do, and we will be obedient.'/

But the people corrupted themselves; they made for themselves a molten calf; and worshiped it.

Ex 24:7, 32:7, 8

LORD, give me ✡ understanding,/
that I may keep thy law
and observe it with my whole heart.

And Moses said, 'Alas, this people have sinned a great sin.'/
But the LORD said, 'Whoever has sinned against me, him will I blot out of my book. But now go, lead the people to the land flowing with milk and honey.'

Ex 32:31, 33, 34; 33:3

LORD, give me ✡ understanding ~

'Behold, the days are coming when I will make a new covenant with the house of Israel./
I will put my law within them, and I will write it upon their hearts.'

Jer 31:31, 33

LORD, give me ✡ understanding ~

'A new heart I will give you, and a new spirit I will put within you;/
and I will take out of your flesh the heart of stone and give you a heart of flesh.'

Ezek 36:26

LORD, give me ✡ understanding ~

I will meditate on thy precepts,
and fix my eyes on thy ways./
I will delight in thy statutes;
I will not forget thy word. Amen.

Psalm 119:15, 16

The Third Meditation

The Incarnation

Our ❀ Father

In the beginning was the Word, and the
Word was with God,/
and the Word was God.

John 1:1

The winter ❀ is past,
the rain is over and gone./
The flowers appear on the earth,
the time for singing has come.

Song 2:11, 12

And in the fullness of time the angel Gabriel
was sent from God to a virgin betrothed
to a man whose name was Joseph;/
and the virgin's name was Mary.

Luke 1:26, 27

The winter ❀ is past ~

'Hail, O favored one, the Lord is with you!/
Blessed are you among women!'

Luke 1:28, 42

The winter ❀ is past ~

But she was greatly troubled at the saying,/
and considered in her mind what sort of
greeting this might be.

Luke 1:29

The winter ❀ is past ~

'Do not be afraid, Mary,/
for you have found favor with God.'

Luke 1:30

The winter ❀ is past ~

'And behold, you will conceive in your womb
and bear a son,/
and you shall call his name Jesus.'

Luke 1:31

The winter ❀ is past ~

'He will be great, and will be called the Son
of the Most High;/
and of his kingdom there will be no end.'

Luke 1:32, 33

The winter ❀ is past ~

And Mary said to the angel, 'How shall this
be,/
since I have no husband?'

Luke 1:34

The winter ❀ is past ~

The winter is past,
the rain is over and gone./
The flowers appear on the earth,
the time for singing has come.

'The Holy Spirit will come upon you, and the power of the Most High will overshadow you;/
therefore the child to be born will be called holy, the Son of God.'

Luke 1:35

The winter ❀ is past ~

And Mary said, 'Behold, I am the handmaid of the Lord; let it be to me according to your word.' And the angel departed from her./
And the Word became flesh and dwelt among us.

Lk 1:38; Jn 1:14

The winter ❀ is past ~

For God so loved the world
that he gave his only Son,/
that whoever believes in him
should not perish
but have
eternal
life.

John 3:16

Amen.

The Fourth Meditation

The Nativity

Our ✶ Father

In those days Joseph went to Bethlehem with
Mary, who was with child./
And while they were there, the time came
for her to be delivered.

Luke 2:1, 4-6

Sing for joy ✶ O heavens,
and exult, O earth;
break forth, O mountains, into singing!/
For the Lord has comforted his people.

Isaiah 49:13

And she gave birth to her first-born son/
and wrapped him in swaddling cloths.

Luke 2:7

Sing for joy ✶ O heavens ~

And she laid him in a manger,/
because there was no place for them in
the inn.

Luke 2:7

Sing for joy ✶ O heavens ~

And in that region there were shepherds out in the field, keeping watch over their flock by night./
And an angel of the Lord appeared to them, and the glory of the Lord shone around them.

Luke 2:8, 9

Sing for joy ✶ O heavens ~

'Be not afraid; for behold, I bring you good news of a great joy/
which will come to all the people.'

Luke 2:10

Sing for joy ✶ O heavens ~

'For to you is born this day a Savior,/
who is Christ the Lord.'

Luke 2:11

Sing for joy ✶ O heavens ~

And suddenly there was with the angel a multitude of the heavenly host praising God and saying,/
'Glory to God in the highest, and on earth peace among men with whom he is pleased!'

Luke 2:13 14

Sing for joy ✶ O heavens ~

Sing for joy, O heavens,
and exult, O earth;
break forth O mountains, into singing!/
For the LORD has comforted his people.

And behold, wise men from the East came,/
and going in they saw the child with Mary
his mother.

Matt 2:1, 11

Sing for joy ✶ O heavens ~

And they fell down and worshiped him./
Then, opening their treasures, they offered
him gifts, gold and frankincense and
myrrh.

Matt 2:11

Sing for joy ✶ O heavens ~

And the child grew and became strong, filled
with wisdom;/
and the favor of God was upon him.

Luke 2:40

Sing for joy ✶ O heavens ~

And the darkness
is passing away,/
and the true light
is already
shining.

1 John 2:8

Amen.

The Fifth Meditation

THE PRECURSOR

Our Father

In those days John the Baptist appeared in the wilderness of Judea,/
preaching, 'Prepare the way of the Lord.'
Mt 3:1, 3; Mk 1:4

Hear the voice of
one crying in the wilderness;/
to give light to those
who sit in darkness,
and to guide our feet
into the way of peace.
Luke 3:4; 1:79

'Make his paths straight,/
for I tell you, even now the axe is laid to the root of the trees.'
Matt 3:3, 9, 10

Hear the voice of ~

'Every tree therefore that does not bear good fruit/
is cut down and thrown into the fire.'
Luke 3:9

Hear the voice of ~

And the multitudes asked him, 'What then shall we do?'/
And John answered them, 'He who has two coats, let him share with him who has none.'

Luke 3:10, 11

Hear the voice of ~

'And he who has food,/
let him do likewise.'

Luke 3:11

Hear the voice of ~

And he preached, saying, 'After me comes he who is mightier than I,/
the thong of whose sandals I am not worthy to stoop down and untie.'

Mark 1:7

Hear the voice of ~

'I have baptized you with water;/
but he will baptize you with the Holy Spirit and with fire.'

Mk 1:8; Lk 3:16

Hear the voice of ~

Hear the voice of
one crying in the wilderness;/
to give light to those
who sit in darkness,
and to guide our feet
into the way of peace.

The next day he saw Jesus coming toward him,/
and John said, 'Behold, the Lamb of God,
who takes away the sin of the world!'
John 1:29

Hear the voice of ~

And Jesus was baptized by John in the Jordan./
And when he came up out of the water, the
heavens were opened.
Mt 3:16; Mk 1:9, 10

Hear the voice of ~

And the Holy Spirit descended upon him like
a dove,/
and a voice came from heaven saying,
'This is my beloved Son, with whom
I am well pleased.'
Lk 3:22; Mk 1:10, 11; Mt 3:17

Hear the voice of ~

The crooked shall be made straight,
and the rough ways
shall be made smooth;/
and all flesh shall see
the salvation of God.
Luke 3:5, 6

Amen.

Part II The Metanoia

The Sixth Meditation — THE TEMPTATION IN THE WILDERNESS

The Seventh Meditation — MIRACLES

The Eighth Meditation — THE BEATITUDES

The Ninth Meditation — LOVE

The Tenth Meditation — COMPASSION

The Sixth Meditation

The Temptation in the Wilderness

Our ✠ Father

Then Jesus returned from the Jordan,/
and was led by the Spirit into the wilderness to be tempted by the devil.

Lk 4:1; Mt 4:1

Let God ✠ arise,
let his enemies be scattered;/
let those who hate him
flee before him!

Psalm 68:1

And he fasted forty days and forty nights./
And the tempter came and said to him, 'If you are the Son of God, command these stones to become loaves of bread.'

Matt 4:2, 3

Let God ✠ arise ~

But he answered, 'It is written, "Man shall not live by bread alone,/
but by every word that proceeds from the mouth of God." '

Matt 4:4

Let God ✠ arise ~

Then the devil took him to Jerusalem, and set him on the pinnacle of the temple,/
and said to him, 'If you are the Son of God, throw yourself down from here.'

Luke 4:9

Let God ❦ arise ~

'For it is written, "He will give his angels charge of you, to guard you,"/
and "On their hands they will bear you up, lest you strike your foot against a stone." '

Luke 4:10, 11

Let God ❦ arise ~

And Jesus answered him, 'Again it is written,/
"You shall not tempt the Lord your God." '

Lk 4:12; Mt 4:7

Let God ❦ arise ~

Again, the devil took him to a very high mountain,/
and showed him all the kingdoms of the world and the glory of them.

Matt 4:8

Let God ❦ arise ~

Let God arise,
let his enemies be scattered;/
let those who hate him
flee before him!

And he said to him, 'All these I will give you,/
if you will fall down and worship me.'

Matt 4:9

Let God arise ~

Then Jesus said to him, 'Begone, Satan!/
for it is written, "You shall worship the Lord your God and him only shall you serve." '

Matt 4:10

Let God arise ~

And when the devil had ended every temptation, he departed from him until an opportune time./
And behold, angels came and ministered to him.

Lk 4:13; Mt 4:11

Let God arise ~

Come and hear,
all you who fear God,/
and I will tell
what he has done for me.

Psalm 66:16

Amen.

The Seventh Meditation

MIRACLES

Our ℟ Father

Now after John was arrested, Jesus went throughout all Galilee,/
preaching and healing every disease and every infirmity among the people.
Mk 1:14, 39; Mt 4:23

How great are ℟ his signs,
how mighty his wonders!/
O sing to the LORD a new song,
for he has done marvelous things!
Dan 4:3; Ps 98:1

And he entered the synagogue,/
and a man was there who had a withered hand.
Mark 3:1

How great are ℟ his signs ~

And Jesus said to him, 'Stretch out your hand.'/
And he did so, and his hand was restored.
Luke 6:10

How great are ℟ his signs ~

And Bartimaeus, a blind beggar, came to Jesus/
and said to him, 'Master, let me receive my sight.'

Mark 10:46, 50, 51

How great are his signs ~

And Jesus said to him, 'Receive your sight; your faith has made you well.'/
And immediately he received his sight and followed him, glorifying God.

Luke 18:42, 43

How great are his signs ~

And the people were astonished, and said, 'Where did this man get this wisdom and these mighty works?/
Is not this the carpenter?'

Mt 13:54; Mk 6:3

How great are his signs ~

And as Jesus drew near to the gate of a city called Nain,/
behold, a man who had died was being carried out.

Luke 7:11, 12

How great are his signs ~

How great are his signs,
how mighty his wonders!/
O sing to the LORD a new song,
for he has done marvelous things!

He was the only son of his mother, and she was a widow./
And Jesus had compassion on her and said to her, 'Do not weep.'

Luke 7:12, 13

How great are ℟ his signs ~

And he came and touched the bier, and the bearers stood still./
And he said, 'Young man, I say to you, arise.'

Luke 7:14

How great are ℟ his signs ~

And the dead man sat up, and began to speak. And he gave him to his mother./
And at once his fame spread everywhere throughout Galilee.

Lk 7:15; Mk 1:28

How great are ℟ his signs ~

For he stands
at the right hand of the needy,/
and he does not forget
the cry of the afflicted.

Psalm 109:31; 9:12

Amen.

The Eighth Meditation

The Beatitudes

Our ~ Father

Now Jesus went about among the villages,
preaching, 'The time is fulfilled, and
the kingdom of God is at hand;/
repent, and believe in the gospel.'
Mk 6:6; 1:14, 15

Whoever ~ is wise,
let him understand these things;/
for he came that we may have life,
and have it abundantly.
Hos 14:9; Jn 10:10

And he taught them, saying, 'Blessed are
the poor in spirit,/
for theirs is the kingdom of heaven.'
Matt 5:2, 3

Whoever ~ is wise ~

'Blessed are those who mourn,/
for they shall be comforted.'

Matt 5:4

Whoever ∾ is wise ~

'Blessed are the meek,/
for they shall inherit the earth.'

Matt 5:5

Whoever ∾ is wise ~

'Blessed are those who hunger and thirst for righteousness,/
for they shall be satisfied.'

Matt 5:6

Whoever ∾ is wise ~

'Blessed are the merciful,/
for they shall obtain mercy.'

Matt 5:7

Whoever ∾ is wise ~

'Blessed are the pure in heart,/
for they shall see God.'

Matt 5:8

Whoever ∾ is wise ~

Whoever is wise,
let him understand these things;/
for he came that we may have life,
and have it abundantly.

'Blessed are the peacemakers,/
for they shall be called sons of God.'

Matt 5:9

Whoever is wise ~

'Blessed are those who are persecuted for righteousness' sake,/
for theirs is the kingdom of heaven'

Matt 5:10

Whoever is wise ~

And the crowds were astonished at his teaching,/
for he taught them as one who had authority.

Matt 7:28, 29

Whoever is wise ~

Put on then, as God's chosen ones,
compassion, kindness, lowliness,
meekness, and patience./
And above all these put on love,
which binds everything together
in perfect harmony.

Col 3:12, 14

Amen.

The Ninth Meditation

Love

Our ꕥ Father

Jesus declared, 'A new commandment I give
to you, that you love one another;/
even as I have loved you.'

John 13:34

Let all that ꕥ you do be
done in love,/
and you will have joy and gladness.

1 Cor 16:14; Lk 1:14

'So whatever you wish that men would do to
you, do so to them;/
for this is the law and the prophets.'

Matt 7:12

Let all that ꕥ you do be ~

'Love your enemies,/
do good to those who hate you.'

Luke 6:27

Let all that ꕥ you do be ~

'Bless those who curse you,/
pray for those who abuse you.'

Luke 6:28

Let all that ♡ you do be ~

'For if you love those who love you, what credit is that to you?/
For even sinners love those who love them.'

Luke 6:32

Let all that ♡ you do be ~

'And if you do good to those who do good to you, what credit is that to you?/
For even sinners do the same.'

Luke 6:33

Let all that ♡ you do be ~

'But love your enemies, and do good,/
expecting nothing in return.'

Luke 6:35

Let all that ♡ you do be ~

Let all that you do be
done in love,/
and you will have joy and gladness.

'And your reward will be great,/
and you will be sons of the Most High.'
Luke 6:35

Let all that ❀ you do be ~

'For he is kind to the ungrateful and the selfish./
and makes his sun rise on the evil and on the good.'
Lk 6:35; Mt 5:45

Let all that ❀ you do be ~

'You, therefore, must be perfect,/
as your heavenly Father is perfect.'
Matt 5:48

Let all that ❀ you do be ~

Love is patient and kind;
love is not jealous or boastful;
it is not arrogant or rude.
Love does not insist on its own way;
it is not irritable or resentful./
Love bears all things,
believes all things,
hopes all things, endures all things.
Love never ends. Amen.
1 Cor 13:4, 5, 7, 8

The Tenth Meditation

COMPASSION

Our ❦ Father

One day a lawyer asked, 'Teacher, what shall
I do to inherit eternal life?'
Jesus said, 'What is written in the law?
How do you read?'

Luke 10:25, 26

Teach me ❦ thy way,
O LORD,/
that I may walk in thy truth.

Psalm 86·11

He answered, 'You shall love the Lord your
God with all your heart, and with all
your soul, and with all your mind, and
with all your strength;/
and you shall love your neighbor as your-
self.'

Lk 10:27; Mk 12:30, 31

Teach me ❦ thy way ~

Jesus said, 'You have answered right;/
do this, and you will live.'

Luke 10:28

Teach me ❦ thy way ~

But he said, 'And who is my neighbor?'/
Jesus replied, 'On the road to Jericho a man fell among robbers, who stripped him and beat him, and departed, leaving him half dead.'

Luke 10:29, 30

Teach me ❦ thy way ~

'Now by chance a priest was going down that road;/
and when he saw him he passed by on the other side.'

Luke 10:31

Teach me ❦ thy way ~

'But a Samaritan, as he journeyed, saw him, and he had compassion,/
and went to him and bound up his wounds, pouring on oil and wine.'

Luke 10:33, 34

Teach me ❦ thy way ~

'Then he set him on his own beast and brought him to an inn,/
and took care of him.'

Luke 10:34

Teach me ❦ thy way ~

Teach me thy way,
O LORD,/
that I may walk in thy truth.

'And the next day he took out two denarii
and gave them to the innkeeper,/
saying, "Take care of him." '

Luke 10:35

Teach me ❦ thy way ~

' "And whatever more you spend, I will repay
you when I come back."/
Which of these, do you think, proved
neighbor to the man who fell among
the robbers?'

Luke 10:35, 36

Teach me ❦ thy way ~

He said, 'The one who showed mercy on him.'/
And Jesus said to him, 'Go and do likewise.'

Luke 10:37

Teach me ❦ thy way ~

Thy word is a lamp
to my feet/
and a light
to my
path.

Psalm 119:105

Amen.

Part III The Paradox

The Eleventh Meditation PROVIDENCE

The Twelfth Meditation SUBMISSION AND FORGIVENESS

The Thirteenth Meditation RICHES

The Fourteenth Meditation ALMSGIVING

The Fifteenth Meditation PRAYER

The Eleventh Meditation

Providence

Our ❦ Father

Jesus said, 'Come to me, all who labor and are heavy laden,/
and I will give you rest.'

Matt 11:28

Our hearts were ❦ made for thee,
O Lord,/
and will never be at rest
until they rest in thee.

Augustine of Hippo

'Take my yoke upon you, and learn from me;/
for I am gentle and lowly in heart.'

Matt 11:29

Our hearts were ❦ made for thee ~

'And you will find rest for your souls./
For my yoke is easy, and my burden is light.'

Matt 11:29 30

Our hearts were ❦ made for thee ~

'In the world you have tribulation; but be of good cheer./
I have overcome the world.'
John 16:33
Our hearts were made for thee ~

'Therefore I tell you, do not be anxious about your life, what you shall eat or what you shall drink,/
nor about your body, what you shall put on.'
Matt 6:25
Our hearts were made for thee ~

'For all the nations of the world seek these things;/
and your Father knows that you need them.'
Luke 12:30
Our hearts were made for thee ~

'But seek first his kingdom and his righteousness,/
and all these things shall be yours as well.'
Matt 6:33
Our hearts were made for thee ~

Our hearts were made for thee,
O LORD,/
and will never be at rest
until they rest in thee.

'Look at the birds of the air: they neither sow
nor reap nor gather into barns,/
and yet your heavenly Father feeds them.'
Matt 6:26
Our hearts were made for thee ~

'And consider the lilies of the field, how they grow;/
they neither toil nor spin; yet I tell you, even Solomon in all his glory was not arrayed like one of these.'
Matt 6:28, 29
Our hearts were made for thee ~

'Therefore do not be anxious about tomorrow, for tomorrow will be anxious for itself./
Let the day's own trouble be sufficient for the day.'
Matt 6:34
Our hearts were made for thee ~

For even though I walk
through the valley
of the shadow of death,
I fear no evil,/
for thou art with me, O Lord. Amen.
Psalm 23:4

The Twelfth Meditation

SUBMISSION AND FORGIVENESS

Our ✠ Father

'You have heard that it was said, "An eye for
an eye and a tooth for a tooth."/
But I say to you, Do not resist one who
is evil.'

Matt 5:38, 39

O the depth ✠ of the riches
and wisdom and knowledge of God!/
How unsearchable are his judgments
and how inscrutable his ways!

Rom 11:33

'If any one strikes you on the right cheek,/
turn to him the other also.'

Matt 5:39

O the depth ✠ of the riches ~

'And if any one would sue you and take
your coat,/
let him have your cloak as well.'

Matt 5:40

O the depth ✠ of the riches ~

'And if any one forces you to go one mile,/
go with him two miles.'

Matt 5.41

O the depth ✠ of the riches ~

'Judge not, and you will not be judged; condemn not, and you will not be condemned;/
forgive, and you will be forgiven.'

Luke 6:37

O the depth ✠ of the riches ~

'For if you forgive men their trespasses,/
your heavenly Father also will forgive you.'

Matt 6:14

O the depth ✠ of the riches ~

'But if you do not forgive men their trespasses,/
neither will your Father forgive your trespasses.'

Matt 6:15

O the depth ✠ of the riches ~

O the depth of the riches
and wisdom and knowledge of God!
How unsearchable are his judgments
and how inscrutable his ways!

Then Peter said, 'Lord, how often shall my brother sin against me, and I forgive him?/
As many as seven times?'

Matt 18:21

O the depth ✠ of the riches ~

Jesus said to him, 'I do not say to you seven times,/
but seventy times seven.'

Matt 18:22

O the depth ✠ of the riches ~

'For by this all men will know that you are my disciples,/
if you have love for one another.'

John 13:35

O the depth ✠ of the riches ~

Therefore I am content with weaknesses,
insults, hardships, persecutions,
and calamities;/
for when I am weak,
then I am
strong.

2 Cor 12:10

Amen.

The Thirteenth Meditation

Riches

Our ❖ Father

Jesus declared, 'How hard it is for those who have riches/
to enter the kingdom of God!'

Luke 18:24

Keep your ❖ life free
from love of money,/
for the love of money
is the root of all evils.

Heb 13:5; 1 Tim 6:10

'For it is easier for a camel to go through the eye of a needle/
than for a rich man to enter the kingdom of God.'

Luke 18:25

Keep your ❖ life free ~

When the disciples heard this they were greatly astonished,/
saying, 'Who then can be saved?'

Matt 19:25

Keep your ❖ life free ~

Jesus looked at them and said, 'With men it is impossible, but not with God;/
for all things are possible with God.'

Mark 10:27

Keep your life free ~

And he told them a parable, saying, 'The land of a rich man brought forth plentifully,/
and the rich man thought to himself, "You have ample goods laid up for many years; take your ease, eat, drink, be merry." '

Luke 12:16, 17, 19

Keep your life free ~

'But God said to him, "Fool! This night your soul is required of you."/
So is he who lays up treasure for himself, and is not rich toward God.'

Luke 12:20, 21

Keep your life free ~

'Take heed, and beware of all covetousness;/
for a man's life does not consist in the abundance of his possessions.'

Luke 12:15

Keep your life free ~

Keep your life free
from love of money,/
for the love of money
is the root of all evils.

'For you say, I am rich, I have prospered, and I need nothing;/
not knowing that you are wretched, pitiable, poor, blind, and naked.'

Rev 3:17

Keep your life free ~

Now the Pharisees, who were lovers of money, heard all this, and they scoffed at him./
But he said to them, 'You are those who justify yourselves before men.'

Luke 16:14, 15

Keep your life free ~

'But God knows your hearts;/
for what is exalted among men is an abomination in the sight of God.'

Luke 16:15

Keep your life free ~

Be content with what you have;/
for has not God chosen those who are
poor in the world to be rich in faith
and heirs of the kingdom
which he has promised
to those who love him? Amen.

Heb 13:5; Jas 2:5

The Fourteenth Meditation

ALMSGIVING

Our Father

Jesus said, 'It is more blessed to give/
than to receive.'

Acts 20:35

Pour yourself out for the hungry
and satisfy the desire of the afflicted,/
then shall your light
rise in the darkness
and your gloom be as the noonday.

Isaiah 58:10

'Therefore, do not lay up for yourselves treasures on earth,/
where moth and rust consume and where thieves break in and steal.'

Matt 6:19

Pour yourself out for the hungry ~

'But lay up for yourselves treasure in heaven,/
where neither moth nor rust consumes and where thieves do not break in and steal.'

Matt 6:20

Pour yourself out for the hungry ~

'For where your treasure is,/
there will your heart be also.'

Matt 6:21

Pour yourself out ❧ for the hungry ~

'Give to every one who begs from you;/
and do not refuse him who would borrow from you.'

Lk 6:30; Mt 5:42

Pour yourself out ❧ for the hungry ~

'And when you give a feast, invite the poor, the maimed, the lame, the blind,/
and you will be blessed, because they cannot repay you.'

Luke 14:13, 14

Pour yourself out ❧ for the hungry ~

'Give, and it will be given to you;/
good measure, pressed down, shaken together, running over, will be put into your lap.'

Luke 6:38

Pour yourself out ❧ for the hungry ~

Pour yourself out for the hungry
and satisfy the desire of the afflicted,/
then shall your light
rise in the darkness
and your gloom be as the noonday.

'For the measure you give will be the measure
you get back./
You will be repaid at the resurrection of
the just.'

Luke 6:38; 14:14

Pour yourself out ❧ for the hungry ~

'But when you give alms,/
do not let your left hand know what your
right hand is doing.'

Matt 6:3

Pour yourself out ❧ for the hungry ~

'So that your alms may be in secret;/
and your Father who sees in secret will
reward you.'

Matt 6:4

Pour yourself out ❧ for the hungry ~

For if any one has the world's goods
and sees his brother in need,
yet closes his heart against him,/
how does God's love
abide in
him?

1 John 3:17

Amen.

The Fifteenth Meditation

Prayer

Our Father

'Ask, and it will be given you; seek, and you will find;/
knock, and it will be opened to you.'

Matt 7:7

Pray at all times;/
draw near to God
and he will draw near to you.

Eph 6:18; Jas 4:8

'For every one who asks receives, and he who seeks finds,/
and to him who knocks it will be opened.'

Matt 7:8

Pray at all times ~

'Or what man of you, if his son asks him for bread, will give him a stone?/
Or if he asks for a fish, will give him a serpent?'

Matt 7:9, 10

Pray at all times ~

'If you then give good gifts to your children,/
how much more will your Father who is in heaven give good things to those who ask him!'

Matt 7:11

Pray at all times ~

'But not every one who says to me, "Lord, Lord," shall enter the kingdom of heaven,/
but he who does the will of my Father who is in heaven.'

Matt 7:21

Pray at all times ~

'And in praying do not heap up empty phrases as the Gentiles do;/
for they think that they will be heard for their many words.'

Matt 6:7

Pray at all times ~

'Do not be like them,/
for your Father knows what you need before you ask him.'

Matt 6:8

Pray at all times ~

Pray at all times;/
draw near to God
and he will draw near to you.

'And when you fast, do not look dismal, like the hypocrites,/
for they disfigure their faces that their fasting may be seen by men.'

Matt 6:16

Pray at all times ~

'But when you fast, wash your face, that your fasting may not be seen by men but by your Father who is in secret;/
and your Father who sees in secret will reward you.'

Matt 6:17, 18

Pray at all times ~

'And whatever you ask in prayer, you will receive, if you have faith./
But apart from me you can do nothing.'

Mt 21:22; Jn 15:5

Pray at all times ~

Set your minds
on things that are above,
not on things that are on earth./
And let the peace of Christ
rule in your hearts. Amen.

Col 3:2, 15

Part IV The Challenge

The Sixteenth Meditation PERSECUTION

The Seventeenth Meditation SIN

The Eighteenth Meditation CONVERSION

The Nineteenth Meditation MARRIAGE

The Twentieth Meditation APOSTLESHIP

The Sixteenth Meditation
PERSECUTION
Our ❦ Father

'Blessed are you when men hate you,/
and when they exclude you and revile you
on account of the Son of man!'
Luke 6:22

The LORD is ❦ my light
and my salvation;/
whom shall I fear?
Psalm 27:1

'Rejoice in that day, and leap for joy,/
for behold, your reward is great in heaven.'
Luke 6:23
The LORD is ❦ my light ~

'If the world hates you,/
know that it has hated me before it hated you.'
John 15:18
The LORD is ❦ my light ~

'If you were of the world,/
the world would love its own.'

John 15:19

The LORD is my light ~

'But because you are not of the world, but
I chose you out of the world,/
therefore, the world hates you.'

John 15:19

The LORD is my light ~

'They will lay their hands on you and persecute you,/
delivering you up to the prisons.'

Luke 21:12

The LORD is my light ~

'And you will be hated by all for my name's sake./
But he who endures to the end will be saved.'

Mark 13:13

The LORD is my light ~

The LORD is my light
and my salvation;/
whom shall I fear?

'So every one who acknowledges me before men,/
I also will acknowledge before my Father who is in heaven.'

Matt 10:32

The LORD is ❧ my light ~

'But whoever denies me before men,/
I also will deny before my Father who is in heaven.'

Matt 10:33

The LORD is ❧ my light ~

'Therefore do not fear those who kill the body but cannot kill the soul;/
rather fear him who can destroy both soul and body in hell.'

Matt 10:28

The LORD is ❧ my light ~

Though a host encamp against me,
my heart shall not fear,/
for the sufferings of this present time
are not worth comparing with the glory
that is to be revealed in us.

Ps 27:3; Rom 8:18

Amen.

The Seventeenth Meditation

Sin

Our Father

'Strive to enter by the narrow gate; for the gate is wide and the way is easy, that leads to destruction,/
and those who enter by it are many.'
Lk 13:24; Mt 7:13

Out of the depths I cry to thee,
O Lord!/
Lord, hear my voice!
Psalm 130:1, 2

'But the gate is narrow and the way is hard, that leads to life,/
and those who find it are few.'
Matt 7:14

Out of the depths I cry to thee ~

'For out of the heart of man, come evil thoughts,/
fornication, theft, murder, adultery.'
Mark 7:21

Out of the depths I cry to thee ~

'Coveting, wickedness, deceit, licentiousness, envy, slander, pride, foolishness./
All these things defile a man.'

Mark 7:22, 23

Out of the depths ▣ I cry to thee ~

'Therefore if your eye causes you to sin, pluck it out;/
it is better for you to enter the kingdom of God with one eye than with two eyes to be thrown into hell.'

Mark 9:47

Out of the depths ▣ I cry to thee ~

'And if your hand causes you to sin, cut it off;/
it is better for you to enter life maimed than with two hands to go to the unquenchable fire.'

Mark 9:43

Out of the depths ▣ I cry to thee ~

'You have heard, "You shall not kill."/
But I say to you that every one who is angry with his brother shall be liable to judgment.'

Matt 5:21, 22

Out of the depths ▣ I cry to thee ~

Out of the depths I cry to thee,
O LORD!/
Lord, hear my voice!

'And you have heard, "You shall not commit adultery."/
But I say to you that every one who looks at a woman lustfully has already committed adultery with her in his heart.'
Matt 5:27, 28
Out of the depths ▣ I cry to thee ~

'And woe to you who outwardly appear righteous to men/
but within are full of hypocrisy and iniquity.'
Matt 23:27, 28
Out of the depths ▣ I cry to thee ~

'Hypocrites! You are like whitewashed tombs, which outwardly appear beautiful,/
but within they are full of dead men's bones and all uncleanness.'
Matt 23:27
Out of the depths ▣ I cry to thee ~

Bring me back, for I have strayed,
bind me up, for I am crippled,/
strengthen me, O LORD, for I am weak.
Ezek 34:16

Amen.

The Eighteenth Meditation

Conversion

Our Father

'Some men hear the word of the kingdom
but do not understand it,/
then the devil comes and takes away the word from their hearts.'

Mt 13:19; Lk 8:12

Seek the LORD
while he may be found,
call upon him while he is near;/
that he may come
and rain salvation upon you.

Is 55:6; Hos 10:12

'Others hear the word and receive it with joy;/
they believe for a while but in time of temptation fall away.'

Luke 8:13

Seek the LORD ~

'Still others hear, but as they go on their way they are choked by the cares and riches and pleasures of life,/
and their fruit does not mature.'

Luke 8:14

Seek the LORD ~

'But also there are those who, hearing the word, hold it fast in an honest and good heart,/
and bring forth fruit with patience.'

Luke 8:15

Seek the LORD ~

'Behold, I stand at the door and knock;/
if any one hears my voice and opens the door, I will come in.'

Rev 3:20

Seek the LORD ~

'But do not think that I have come to bring peace on earth;/
I have not come to bring peace, but a sword.'

Matt 10:34

Seek the LORD ~

'For I have come to set a man against his father, and a daughter against her mother;/
and a man's foes will be those of his own household.'

Matt 10:35, 36

Seek the LORD ~

Seek the LORD
while he may be found,
call upon him while he is near;/
that he may come
and rain salvation upon you.

'For he who loves father or mother more
than me/
is not worthy of me.'

Matt 10:37

Seek the ❦ LORD ~

'He who is not with me is against me;/
and he who does not gather with me
scatters.'

Luke 11:23

Seek the ❦ LORD ~

'I came to cast fire upon the earth;/
and would that it were already kindled!'

Luke 12:49

Seek the ❦ LORD ~

And be doers of the word,
and not hearers only,
deceiving yourselves./
For whoever knows
what is right to do
and fails to do it,
for him it is
a sin.

James 1:22; 4:17

Amen.

The Nineteenth Meditation

Marriage

Our ♡ Father

One day Pharisees asked, 'Is it lawful for a man to divorce his wife?'/
Jesus said, 'From the beginning of creation, "God made them male and female." '

Mark 10:2, 6

Lord, grant that ♡ I may seek
not so much to be consoled,
as to console;/
to be understood, as to understand;
to be loved, as to love.

Francis of Assisi

'For this reason a man shall leave his father and mother and be joined to his wife,/
and the two shall become one flesh.'

Mark 10:7, 8

Lord, grant that ♡ I may seek ~

'So they are no longer two but one flesh./
What therefore God has joined together, let not man put asunder.'

Mark 10:8, 9

Lord, grant that ♡ I may seek ~

They said to him, 'Why then did Moses allow
a man to write a certificate of divorce,/
and put her away?'

Mt 19:7; Mk 10:4

Lord, grant that I may seek ~

'For your hardness of heart Moses allowed
you to divorce your wives,/
but from the beginning it was not so.'

Matt 19:8

Lord, grant that I may seek ~

'And I say to you: whoever divorces his wife
and marries another,/
commits adultery against her.'

Mark 10:11

Lord, grant that I may seek ~

'And if she divorces her husband and marries
another,/
she commits adultery.'

Mark 10:12

Lord, grant that I may seek ~

LORD, grant that I may seek
not so much to be consoled,
as to console;/
to be understood, as to understand;
to be loved, as to love.

The disciples said, 'If such is the case, it is not expedient to marry.'/
Jesus said, 'Not all men can receive this saying, but only those to whom it is given.'

Matt 19:10, 11

LORD, grant that ♡ I may seek ~

'For there are eunuchs who have been so from birth,/
and there are eunuchs who have been made eunuchs by men.'

Matt 19:12

LORD, grant that ♡ I may seek ~

'And there are eunuchs who have made themselves eunuchs for the sake of the kingdom of heaven./
He who is able to receive this, let him receive it.'

Matt 19:12

LORD, grant that ♡ I may seek ~

For it is in giving that we receive;
it is in pardoning that we are pardoned;/
it is in dying
that we are born to eternal life. Amen.

Francis of Assisi

The Twentieth Meditation

Apostleship

Our ❧ Father

Jesus said, 'The harvest is plentiful, but the
laborers are few;/
pray therefore the Lord of the harvest to
send out laborers into his harvest.'
Luke 10:2

How beautiful upon ❧ the mountains/
are the feet of those who preach
the good news of salvation!
Is 52:7; Rom 10:15

And he saw Levi sitting at the tax office,
and he said to him, 'Follow me.'/
And he rose and followed him.
Mark 2:14

How beautiful upon ❧ the mountains ~

And a man asked him, 'Teacher, what good
deed must I do, to have eternal life?'/
Jesus said to him, 'If you would enter
life, keep the commandments.'
Matt 19:16, 17

How beautiful upon ❧ the mountains ~

'Teacher, all these I have observed from my youth.'/
And Jesus looking upon him loved him, and said to him, 'You lack one thing.'

Mark 10:20, 21

How beautiful upon ❧ the mountains ~

'Go, sell all that you have, and give to the poor, and you will have treasure in heaven;/
and come, follow me.'

Mk 10:21; Lk 18:22

How beautiful upon ❧ the mountains ~

At that saying his countenance fell, and he went away sorrowful;/
for he was very rich.

Mk 10:22; Lk 18:23

How beautiful upon ❧ the mountains ~

Then Peter said, 'We have left everything and followed you./
What then shall we have?'

Matt 19:27

How beautiful upon ❧ the mountains ~

How beautiful upon the mountains/
are the feet of those who preach
the good news of salvation!

'Every one who has left houses or brothers
or sisters or father or mother or children
or lands, for my sake, will receive a
hundredfold now in this time,/
and in the age to come eternal life.'

Mt 19:29; Mk 10:29, 30

How beautiful upon ❧ the mountains ~

'For whoever would save his life will lose it;/
and whoever loses his life for my sake will
find it.'

Matt 16:25

How beautiful upon ❧ the mountains ~

'For what will it profit a man, if he gains the
whole world and forfeits his life?/
Or what shall a man give in return for his
life?'

Matt 16:26

How beautiful upon ❧ the mountains ~

For how are men to believe
in him of whom they have never heard?/
And how are they to hear
without a preacher? Amen.

Rom 10:14

Part V The Climax

The Twenty-first Meditation	THE KINGDOM OF GOD
The Twenty-second Meditation	THE CHURCH
The Twenty-third Meditation	THE EUCHARIST
The Twenty-fourth Meditation	THE PASSION
The Twenty-fifth Meditation	THE CRUCIFIXION

The Twenty-first Meditation

The Kingdom of God

Our Father

Jesus said, 'The kingdom of God is like treasure hidden in a field, which a man found and covered up;/
then in his joy he goes and sells all that he has and buys that field.'

Matt 13:44

One thing have I asked of the LORD,
that will I seek after;/
that I may dwell in the house
of the LORD all the days of my life.

Psalm 27:4

'Again, the kingdom of God is like a merchant in search of fine pearls,/
who, on finding one pearl of great value, went and sold all that he had and bought it.'

Matt 13:45, 46

One thing have I asked of the LORD ~

'The kingdom of God is in the midst of you./
Therefore walk while you have the light, lest the darkness overtake you.'

Lk 17:21; Jn 12:35

One thing have I asked of the LORD ~

'And let your light so shine before men,
that they may see your good works/
and give glory to your Father who is in
heaven.'

Matt 5:16

One thing have I asked of the LORD ~

'And when you have done all that is commanded you, say, "We are unworthy servants;/
we have only done what was our duty." '

Luke 17:10

One thing have I asked of the LORD ~

'For every one to whom much is given,/
of him will much be required.'

Luke 12:48

One thing have I asked of the LORD ~

'And no one who puts his hand to the plow
and looks back/
is fit for the kingdom of God.'

Luke 9:62

One thing have I asked of the LORD ~

One thing have I asked of the LORD,
that will I seek after;/
that I may dwell
in the house of the LORD
all the days of my life.

And calling to him a child, and taking him in his arms,/
Jesus said, 'To such belongs the kingdom of God.'

Mt 18:2; Mk 9:36; 10:14

One thing have I asked of the LORD ~

'Truly, I say to you, whoever does not receive the kingdom of God like a child/
shall not enter it.'

Mark 10:15

One thing have I asked of the LORD ~

And Jesus declared, 'I thank thee, Father, that thou hast hidden these things from the wise and understanding and revealed them to babes;/
for such was thy gracious will.'

Matt 11:25, 26

One thing have I asked of the LORD ~

For his kingdom
is an everlasting kingdom,/
and his dominion
is from generation to generation.

Daniel 4:3

Amen.

The Twenty-second Meditation

THE CHURCH

Our ✠ Father

In those days Jesus asked his disciples, 'Who do you say that I am?'/
Simon Peter replied, 'You are the Christ, the Son of the living God.'

Matt 16:13, 15, 16

Let all ✠ mankind
call on the name of the LORD/
and serve him with one accord.

Zeph 1:3, 3:9

And Jesus answered him, 'Blessed are you, Simon Bar-Jona!/
For flesh and blood has not revealed this to you, but my Father who is in heaven.'

Matt 16:17

Let all ✠ mankind ~

'And I tell you, you are Peter, and on this rock I will build my church,/
and the powers of death shall not prevail against it.'

Matt 16:18

Let all ✠ mankind ~

'I will give you the keys of the kingdom of heaven,/
and whatever you bind on earth shall be bound in heaven, and whatever you loose on earth shall be loosed in heaven.'

Matt 16:19

Let all ✠ mankind ~

And Jesus said to his disciples, 'If you forgive the sins of any, they are forgiven;/
if you retain the sins of any, they are retained.'

John 20:23

Let all ✠ mankind ~

'Again I say to you, if two of you agree on earth about anything they ask,/
it will be done for them by my Father in heaven.'

Matt 18:19

Let all ✠ mankind ~

'For where two or three are gathered in my name,/
there am I in the midst of them.'

Matt 18:20

Let all ✠ mankind ~

Let all mankind
call on the name of the LORD/
and serve him with one accord.

'I am the good shepherd; my sheep hear my voice, and they follow me;/
and I give them eternal life.'

John 10:14, 27, 28

Let all ✠ mankind ~

'And I have other sheep, that are not of this fold;/
I must bring them also.'

John 10:16

Let all ✠ mankind ~

'And they will heed my voice./
So there shall be one flock, one shepherd.'

John 10:16

Let all ✠ mankind ~

And let us
stir up one another
to love
and
good works,/
not neglecting
to meet
together.

Heb 10:24, 25

Amen.

The Twenty-third Meditation

THE EUCHARIST

Our Father

Jesus said to his disciples, 'I am the living bread which came down from heaven;/
if any one eats of this bread, he will live for ever.'

John 6:51

Surely goodness and mercy
shall follow me
all the days of my life;/
and I shall dwell
in the house of the LORD for ever.

Psalm 23:6

'Truly, truly, I say to you, unless you eat the flesh of the Son of man and drink his blood,/
you have no life in you.'

John 6:53

Surely goodness and mercy ~

'For my flesh is food indeed, and my blood is drink indeed./
He who eats my flesh and drinks my blood abides in me, and I in him.'

John 6:55, 56

Surely goodness and mercy ~

Now after this many of his disciples drew back and no longer went about with him./
And Jesus said to the twelve, 'Do you also wish to go away?'

John 6.66, 67

Surely goodness and mercy ∼

Simon Peter answered him, 'Lord, to whom shall we go?/
You have the words of eternal life.'

John 6:68

Surely goodness and mercy ∼

'And we have believed, and have come to know,/
that you are the Holy One of God.'

John 6:69

Surely goodness and mercy ∼

Now on the night when he was betrayed Jesus took bread,/
and blessed, and broke it.

1 Cor 11:23; Mt 26:26

Surely goodness and mercy ∼

Surely goodness and mercy
shall follow me
all the days of my life;/
and I shall dwell
in the house of the LORD for ever.

And he gave it to the disciples and said,
'Take, eat;/
this is my body.'

Matt 26:26

Surely goodness and mercy ~

And he took a cup, and when he had given
thanks he gave it to them,/
saying, 'Drink of it, all of you.'

Matt 26:27

Surely goodness and mercy ~

'For this is my blood of the new covenant,
which is poured out for many for the
forgiveness of sins./
Do this, in remembrance of me.'

Mt 26:28; 1 Cor 11:25

Surely goodness and mercy ~

For the Lord is my shepherd,
I shall not want;
he makes me lie down
in green pastures./
he leads me beside still waters;
he restores my soul.

Psalm 23:1-3

Amen.

The Twenty-fourth Meditation
THE PASSION

Our ❧ Father

And when they had sung a hymn, they went
out to the Mount of Olives./
And Jesus said, 'My soul is very sorrowful,
even to death.'

Mark 14:26, 34

Sigh therefore ❧ Son of man;/
sigh with breaking heart
and bitter grief before our eyes.

Ezek 21:6

And he prayed, 'Father, if thou art willing,
remove this cup from me;/
yet not my will, but thine, be done.'

Lk 22:42; Mk 14:36

Sigh therefore ❧ Son of man ~

And there appeared to him an angel from
heaven, strengthening him./
And being in agony he prayed more
earnestly.

Luke 22:43, 44

Sigh therefore ❧ Son of man ~

And his sweat became like great drops of blood/
falling down upon the ground.

Luke 22:44

Sigh therefore ❧ Son of man ~

Then Judas came, and with him a crowd with swords and clubs,/
and they seized Jesus and bound him.

Mk 14:43; Jn 18:12

Sigh therefore ❧ Son of man ~

Then Simon Peter drew his sword. But Jesus said, 'Put your sword back into its place;/
for all who take the sword will perish by the sword.'

Jn 18:10; Mt 26:51, 52

Sigh therefore ❧ Son of man ~

And they led Jesus to the high priest,/
and the high priest said to him, 'I adjure you by the living God, tell us if you are the Christ, the Son of God.'

Mk 14:53; Mt 26:63

Sigh therefore ❧ Son of man ~

Sigh therefore, Son of man;/
sigh with breaking heart
and bitter grief before our eyes.

And Jesus said, 'I am.'/
Then the high priest tore his robes, and said, 'He has uttered blasphemy.'
Mk 14:62; Mt 26:65
Sigh therefore ❧ Son of man ~

Then they spat in his face, and struck him./
And the soldiers plaited a crown of thorns, and put it on his head.
Mt 26:67; Jn 19:2
Sigh therefore ❧ Son of man ~

Then Pilate, wishing to satisfy the crowd, took Jesus and scourged him./
And they led him away to crucify him.
Jn 19:1; Mk 15:15; Mt 27:31
Sigh therefore ❧ Son of man ~

For you call
and we do not answer,
you speak
and we do not listen;/
and the LORD has laid upon you
the iniquity of us all.
Isaiah 65:12; 53:6

Amen.

The Twenty-fifth Meditation

THE CRUCIFIXION

Our ✝ Father

They brought Jesus to the place called The
Skull./
and there they crucified him.

Mk 15:22; Lk 23:33

The word of ✝ the cross
is folly
to those who are perishing,/
but to us who are being saved
it is the power of God.

1 Cor 1:18

And Jesus said, 'Father, forgive them;/
for they know not what they do.'

Luke 23:34

The word of ✝ the cross ~

And one of the criminals who were crucified
with him said, 'Jesus, remember me/
when you come into your kingdom.'

Lk 23:39, 42; Mt 27:44

The word of ✝ the cross ~

And Jesus said to him, 'Truly, I say to you,/
today you will be with me in Paradise.'

Luke 23:43

The word of ✝ the cross ~

And there was darkness over the whole land,/
and the earth shook, and the curtain of the temple was torn in two.

Lk 23:44, 45; Mt 27:51

The word of ✝ the cross ~

And Jesus uttered a loud cry,/
saying, 'Father, into thy hands I commit my spirit!'

Mk 15:37; Lk 23:46

The word of ✝ the cross ~

And he bowed his head/
and breathed his last.

Jn 19:30; Mk 15:37

The word of ✝ the cross ~

And one of the soldiers pierced his side with a spear,/
and at once there came out blood and water.

John 19:34

The word of ✝ the cross ~

The word of the cross
is folly
to those who are perishing,/
but to us who are being saved
it is the power of God.

Now when the multitudes who had assembled to see the sight saw what had taken place,/
they returned home beating their breasts.

Luke 23:48

The word of ✝ the cross ~

And when the centurion, who stood facing him, saw that he thus breathed his last,/
he said, 'Truly this man was the Son of God!'

Mark 15:39

The word of ✝ the cross ~

For the Son of man came
not be be served
but to serve,/
and to give
his life
as a
ransom
for
many.

Mark 10:45

Amen.

Part VI The Triumph

The Twenty-sixth Meditation

The Resurrection

Our ⁂ Father

Jesus said, 'I am the resurrection and the life;/
he who believes in me, though he die, yet shall he live.'

John 11:25

Let all the ⁂ morning stars
sing together,
and all the sons of God shout for joy,/
for death is swallowed up in victory
through our Lord Jesus Christ.

Job 38:7; 1 Cor 15:54, 57

'And whoever lives and believes in me/
shall never die.'

John 11:26

Let all the ⁂ morning stars ~

Now at early dawn the women went to the tomb to anoint the body of Jesus,/
saying, 'Who will roll away the stone for us from the door of the tomb?'

Lk 24:1; Mk 16:1, 3

Let all the ⁂ morning stars ~

And behold, there was a great earthquake;/
for an angel of the Lord descended from heaven and came and rolled back the stone.

Matt 28:2

Let all the morning stars ~

And the angel said to the women, 'Do not be afraid;/
for I know that you seek Jesus who was crucified.'

Matt 28:5

Let all the morning stars ~

'He is not here; for he has risen from the dead./
Come, see the place where they laid him.'

Mt 28:6, 7; Mk 16:6

Let all the morning stars ~

And on the evening of that day, Jesus came and stood among the disciples,/
and he said to them, 'Peace be with you.'

John 20:19

Let all the morning stars ~

Let all the morning stars
sing together,
and all the sons of God shout for joy,/
for death is swallowed up in victory
through our Lord Jesus Christ.

Thomas was not with them when Jesus came./
And he said, 'Unless I see in his hands the print of the nails, and place my hand in his side, I will not believe.'

John 20:24, 25

Let all the morning stars ~

Eight days later Jesus came again and said to Thomas, 'Put your finger here, and see my hands; and put out your hand, and place it in my side;/
do not be faithless, but believing.'

John 20:26, 27

Let all the morning stars ~

Thomas answered, 'My Lord and my God!'/
Jesus said, 'Have you believed because you have seen me? Blessed are those who have not seen and yet believe.'

John 20:28, 29

Let all the morning stars ~

O death, where is thy victory?
O death, where is thy sting?/
For God will wipe away
every tear from our eyes,
and death shall be no more. Amen.

1 Cor 15:55; Rev 21:4

The Twenty-seventh Meditation

THE ASCENSION

Our ✣ Father

Jesus led his disciples out as far as Bethany;/
and lifting up his hands he blessed them.
Luke 24:50

Know therefore ✣ this day,
and lay it to your heart,/
that the LORD is God in heaven above
and on the earth beneath.
Deut 4:39

Saying, 'All authority in heaven and on earth/
has been given to me.'
Matt 28:18

Know therefore ✣ this day ~

'Go therefore into all the world/
and make disciples of all nations.'

Mt 28:19; Mk 16:15

Know therefore ❁ this day ~

'Baptizing them/
in the name of the Father and of the Son
and of the Holy Spirit.'

Matt 28:19

Know therefore ❁ this day ~

'Teaching them to observe/
all that I have commanded you.'

Matt 28:20

Know therefore ❁ this day ~

'He who believes and is baptized/
will be saved.'

Mark 16:16

Know therefore ❁ this day ~

'But he who does not believe/
will be condemned.'

Mark 16:16

Know therefore ❁ this day ~

Know therefore this day,
and lay it to your heart,/
that the LORD is God in heaven above
and on the earth beneath.

'And lo, I am with you always,/
to the close of the age.'

Matt 28:20

Know therefore ❀ this day ~

And while he blessed them, he was lifted up,/
and a cloud took him out of their sight.

Lk 24:51; Acts 1:9

Know therefore ❀ this day ~

And he was taken up into heaven,/
and sat down at the right hand of God.

Mark 16:19

Know therefore ❀ this day ~

He came to his own home,
and his own people
received him not./
But to all who receive him,
who believe in his name,
he gives power
to become
children
of God.

John 1:11, 12

Amen.

The Twenty-eighth Meditation
PENTECOST
Our ✠ Father

When the day of Pentecost had come, they
were all together in one place,/
devoting themselves to prayer.
Acts 2:1; 1:14

Come, Holy Spirit ✠ fill the hearts
of thy faithful;/
and kindle in them
the fire of thy love.
Anonymous

And suddenly a sound came from heaven/
like the rush of a mighty wind.
Acts 2:2

Come, Holy Spirit ✠ fill the hearts ~

And there appeared to them tongues as of fire,/
distributed and resting on each one of them.
Acts 2:3

Come, Holy Spirit ✠ fill the hearts ~

And they were all filled with the Holy Spirit/
and began to speak of the mighty works of God.

Acts 2:4, 11

Come, Holy Spirit fill the hearts ~

Now there were dwelling in Jerusalem Jews,/
devout men from every nation under heaven.

Acts 2:5

Come, Holy Spirit fill the hearts ~

And Peter, standing with the eleven,/
lifted up his voice and addressed them.

Acts 2:14

Come, Holy Spirit fill the hearts ~

'Men of Israel, save yourselves! Repent, and be baptized every one of you in the name of Jesus Christ for the forgiveness of your sins;/
and you shall receive the gift of the Holy Spirit.'

Acts 2:22, 40, 38

Come, Holy Spirit fill the hearts ~

Come, Holy Spirit, fill the hearts
of thy faithful;/
and kindle in them
the fire of thy love.

So those who received his word were baptized,/
and there were added that day about three thousand souls.

Acts 2:41

Come, Holy Spirit ❦ fill the hearts ~

And they devoted themselves to the apostles' teaching and fellowship,/
to the breaking of bread and the prayers.

Acts 2:42

Come, Holy Spirit ❦ fill the hearts ~

And the disciples went forth and preached everywhere,/
while the Lord worked with them.

Mark 16:20

Come, Holy Spirit ❦ fill the hearts ~

For the night is far gone,
the day is at hand;/
O give thanks
to the LORD,
for he is
good.

Rom 13:12; Ps 136:1

Amen.

The Twenty-ninth Meditation

The Second Coming

Our Father

Jesus said, 'In those days the powers of the heavens will be shaken and there will be signs in sun and moon and stars,/ and upon the earth men fainting with fear of what is coming on the world.'

Luke 21:26, 25

Be patient until the coming of the Lord./
For here we have no lasting city,
but we seek the city which is to come.

Jas 5:7; Heb 13:14

'Now when these things begin to take place, look up and raise your heads,/ because your redemption is drawing near.'

Luke 21:28

Be patient until the ~

'But take heed to yourselves/ lest your hearts be weighed down with dissipation and drunkenness and cares of this life.'

Luke 21:34

Be patient until the ~

'For as it was in the days of Noah,/
so will it be in the days of the Son of man.'

Luke 17:26

Be patient ❀ until the ~

'They were eating and drinking, marrying and giving in marriage,/
and they did not know until the flood came and swept them all away.'

Matt 24:38, 39

Be patient ❀ until the ~

'So will be the coming of the Son of man./
Therefore what I say to you I say to all: Watch.'

Mt 24:39; Mk 13:37

Be patient ❀ until the ~

'Every one then who hears these words of mine and does them/
will be like a wise man who built his house upon the rock.'

Matt 7:24

Be patient ❀ until the ~

Be patient until the
coming of the LORD./
For here we have no lasting city,
but we seek the city which is to come.

'And the rain fell, and the floods came, and the winds blew and beat upon that house,/
but it did not fall, because it had been founded on the rock.'

Matt 7:25

Be patient until the ~

'And every one who hears these words of mine and does not do them/
will be like a foolish man who built his house upon the sand.'

Matt 7:26

Be patient until the ~

'And the rain fell, and the floods came, and the winds blew and beat against that house,/
and it fell; and great was the fall of it.'

Matt 7:27

Be patient until the ~

For the world passes away,
and the lust of it;/
but he who does the will of God
abides for ever.

1 John 2:17

Amen.

The Thirtieth Meditation
The Last Judgment
Our ✠ Father

Jesus said, 'In those days they will see the Son of man coming on the clouds of heaven with power and great glory;/ and he will send out his angels with a loud trumpet call.'

Matt 24:30, 31

No eye has seen ✠ nor ear heard,
nor the heart of man conceived,/
what God has prepared
for those who love him.

1 Cor 2:9

'Before him will be gathered all the nations,/ and he will separate them one from another as a shepherd separates the sheep from the goats.'

Matt 25:32

No eye has seen ✠ nor ear heard ~

'Then he will say to those at his right hand, "Come, O blessed of my Father,/ inherit the kingdom prepared for you from the foundation of the world." '

Matt 25:34

No eye has seen ✠ nor ear heard ~

' "For I was hungry and you gave me food,/
I was thirsty and you gave me drink." '

Matt 25:35

No eye has seen ❋ nor ear heard ~

' "I was a stranger and you welcomed me, I was naked and you clothed me,/
I was sick and you visited me, I was in prison and you came to me." '

Matt 25:35, 36

No eye has seen ❋ nor ear heard ~

' "Lord, when did we see thee hungry, or thirsty,/
or a stranger, or naked, or sick or in prison, and minister to thee?" '

Matt 25:37-39

No eye has seen ❋ nor ear heard ~

' "Truly, I say to you, as you did it to one of the least of these my brethren,/
you did it to me" '

Matt 25:40

No eye has seen ❋ nor ear heard ~

No eye has seen, nor ear heard,
nor the heart of man conceived,/
what God has prepared
for those who love him.

'Then he will say to those at his left hand,
"Depart from me, you cursed,/
into the eternal fire prepared for the devil
and his angels." '

Matt 25:41

No eye has seen ❋ nor ear heard ~

' "For I was hungry, and thirsty, and a stranger,/
and naked, and sick, and in prison, and you did not minister to me." '

Matt 25·42-44

No eye has seen ❋ nor ear heard ~

'And they will go away into eternal punishment,/
but the righteous into eternal life.'

Matt 25:46

No eye has seen ❋ nor ear heard ~

But he who does not love his brother
whom he has seen, cannot love God
whom he has not seen./
And he who does not love
does not know God;
for God is love. Amen.

1 John 4:20, 8

Colophon

This edition of the Christianica, illustrated with 30 golden roundels and marked out with rubrics, has been published by the non-profit Christianica Center.

The roundels were designed in the classic style of ancient Mycenae to suggest the timelessness of the Meditation themes. They were drawn for this book by Cliffe Eitel of Northbrook, Illinois, muralist and designer.

The Meditations have been set in 12 point American Garamond type, an adaptation of the type designed by Claude Garamond of Paris in 1525.

The book has been printed and bound by The Kable Printing Company of Mount Morris, Illinois.

And to the worship of God
has been brought to
completion in the
year of Our Lord
1975 on the
feast of
St. Luke.